For Mom.
Thanks for cheering me on. I love you.
And deep gratitude to Team Sleeping Bear Press—
especially my editor, Sarah Rockett—
for championing this book into the world!
—Elisa

To Becca—
one of my favorite swimmers, who's
not afraid to kick off her socks to
dive into muddy water.
—Elizabeth

 SLEEPING BEAR PRESS™

Text Copyright © 2022 Elisa Boxer
Illustration Copyright © 2022 Elizabeth Baddeley
Design Copyright © 2022 Sleeping Bear Press
All inquiries should be addressed to:
Sleeping Bear Press
2395 South Huron Parkway, Suite 200, Ann Arbor, MI 48104
www.sleepingbearpress.com • © Sleeping Bear Press
Printed and bound in the United States
10 9 8 7 6 5 4 3 2 1
Library of Congress Cataloging-in-Publication Data
Names: Boxer, Elisa, author. | Baddeley, Elizabeth, illustrator.
Title: Splash! : Ethelda Bleibtrey makes waves of change / Elisa Boxer ; Elizabeth Baddeley, Illustrator.
Description: Ann Arbor, MI : Sleeping Bear Press, [2022] | Audience: Ages 6-10 | Summary: "As a child with polio in the early 1900s,
swimming set Ethelda Bleibtrey free. The water released her from her pain and helped her build strong muscle--and a powerful spirit.
From then on, from the New York beaches to the 1920 Olympics, Ethelda made a splash wherever she went"-- Provided by publisher.
Identifiers: LCCN 2022006574 | ISBN 9781534111431 (hardcover) | Subjects: LCSH: Bleibtrey, Ethelda, 1902-1978--Juvenile literature. |
Swimmers--New York (State)--Biography--Juvenile literature. | Olympic athletes--New York (State)--Biography--Juvenile literature. |
Women athletes with disabilities--New York (State)--Biography--Juvenile literature. | Poliomyelitis--Juvenile literature.
Classification: LCC GV838.B55 B69 2022 | DDC 797.2/1092
[B]--dc23/eng/20220225 | LC record available at https://lccn.loc.gov/2022006574

SPLASH!

ETHELDA BLEIBTREY MAKES WAVES OF CHANGE

illustrated by

ELISA BOXER · ELIZABETH BADDELEY

PUBLISHED *by* SLEEPING BEAR PRESS™

BROOKLYN, NEW YORK, 1917

Ethelda's whole body hurt.
Her arms hung heavy.

Sharp pain shot down her legs.
Her spine curved from a disease called polio.
Walking just a few steps left her weak.

Her doctor suggested swimming.

How can I swim when I can barely move? she wondered.

But she was willing to try anything.

The water held her.

Lifted her.

Carried her.

In those moments, something inside of her came alive.

Her heavy limbs felt light.

Her weak muscles felt strong.

It felt like flying.

It felt like freedom.

It felt like home.

"At rest and at peace with the world,"
is how she described her time in the water.

From that place of peace,
Ethelda began to find her power.

Manhattan Beach, New York, 1919

Ethelda was just seventeen years old when she took on the world—by taking off her socks.

The law said women had to wear socks in the water.

Tight, scratchy socks.

No thanks, thought Ethelda.

IF BOYS CAN SWIM WITHOUT SOCKS, SO CAN I.

Boy, did her bare legs make waves.

"YOU'RE UNDER ARREST!"

A policeman handcuffed her, and dragged her right out of the water.

Back then, swimsuit police roamed the beaches with measuring sticks to make sure women's bathing suit bottoms came down low enough, and their socks came up high enough.

Ethelda thought policemen should have far more important things to do than to measure her socks.

She hoped the news of her arrest would spread far and wide. **It did**.

She hoped it would get women talking. **It did**.

And they did.

Everywhere.

Pools . . .

Lakes . . .

Beaches...

The socks came off and the women dove into their newfound freedom.

The police couldn't keep up. So they gave up.

Women were finally free to swim sockless.

All because of one brave girl who dared to test the waters—a girl who, just two years earlier, didn't even know how to swim.

ANTWERP, BELGIUM, 1920

Ethelda, with a curved spine and a competitive spirit, stood still at the start of the race.

No American woman had ever won an Olympic gold medal in swimming.

In fact, many people didn't believe women belonged in the muddy water where the races were held.

Especially without socks.

But Ethelda didn't mind mud.

And she definitely didn't appreciate anyone telling her where she did or did not belong.

When the starting pistol fired off, she dove into the murky muck, where the river met the sea.

The water held her.

Lifted her.

Carried her.

In those moments, something inside of her came alive.

Her limbs felt light.

Her muscles felt strong.

It felt like flying.

It felt like freedom.

It felt like home.

The crowd cheered for Ethelda Bleibtrey, the first American woman ever to win a gold medal in swimming!

But she didn't stop there. . . .

A second gold medal. A third.

Three gold medals and three world records.

The girl who had barely been able to walk without pain became the first woman in the world to win all of the swimming events in a single Olympics.

Back in New York City, Ethelda used her Olympic-sized talent as a coach, but there weren't enough swimming spaces.

SPLASH!

"_NO SWIMMING,_" read the sign at the Central Park Reservoir.
The water covered ten city blocks.
She hoped her splash would get public officials talking. **It did . . .**

And construction soon began on New York City's
first large public swimming pool.

St. Charles Hospital, New York

In the years that followed, Ethelda became a nurse.

Her patients were children.

    Their bodies hurt.

        Their arms hung heavy.

            Sharp pain shot down their legs.

Their spines curved from a disease called polio.
Walking just a few steps left them weak.

Ethelda remembered.

Ethelda dedicated the rest of her life to helping children believe in their bodies.

The water held them.

Lifted them.

Carried them.

In those moments, something inside of them came alive.

Their heavy limbs felt light.

Their weak muscles felt strong.

It felt like flying.

It felt like freedom.

It felt like home.

For Ethelda, too.

ETHELDA BLEIBTREY
WAS A GIRL WITH GUTS WHO LOVED THE WATER.

In 1919, Ethelda Bleibtrey was arrested for nude swimming when she removed her socks before jumping in the water. Can you imagine swimming with your socks? Neither could Ethelda. But back then, sockless females were considered nude. Ethelda saw a situation that didn't feel right, and decided to make a splash. Her biography in the International Swimming Hall of Fame says of the socks incident: "Resulting publicity and public opinion swinging in her favor not only emancipated Ethelda from jail, but women's swimming from stockings."

Beach patrolman measures the distance between a woman's knee and her bathing suit bottom, 1922

Universal History Archive via Getty Images

At a time when women weren't even allowed to vote, Ethelda was changing laws by standing up for something she believed in. It was the first time she used the water as a way to create meaningful change. But it wouldn't be the last.

At the 1920 Olympics, while still a teenager, she entered the only three swimming races open to women that year: the 100-meter freestyle, the 300-meter freestyle, and the 4x100-meter freestyle relay. She won gold medals in all three. Not only did she become America's first female to win an Olympic gold medal in swimming, she also became the only woman ever to win all of the swimming events at any Olympic Games. Just 24 years earlier, the founder of the International Olympic Committee, Pierre de Coubertin, voiced his strong opposition to women participating in sports. "Their primary role should be to crown the victors," he said, later adding that a woman should "encourage her sons to excel rather than seek records for herself."

Ethelda Bleibtrey

International Swimming Hall of Fame Archives

In 1928, Ethelda taught swimming to children with debilitating diseases like polio and cerebral palsy. She realized there weren't enough public swimming pools available to use, so she decided to make a statement by diving into the Central Park Reservoir. A city ordinance prevented swimming there, and Ethelda was arrested yet again. The mayor intervened, Ethelda was released from jail, and New York City's children got their first big public swimming pool.

Helping children find their strength through swimming was a personal mission for Ethelda, who had taken up the sport as a teenager to try to recover from polio. In the water, she found her strength. Swimming became not only a sport, but a way to break barriers.

In 1967, Ethelda was inducted into the International Swimming Hall of Fame. The following year she moved to Florida, where she passed away in 1978, at the age of 76.

I wrote this book when I was housebound for several years, struggling with severe Lyme disease. Having a chronic illness, and being a former competitive swimmer and diver myself, I was especially moved by Ethelda's story. Here was a girl with a debilitating disease who found her strength in the water and used it to overcome obstacles and create social change.

Ethelda Bleibtrey at the 1920 Olympics in Antwerp, Belgium

Popperfoto Collection via Getty Images

"At rest and at peace with the world" is how she described her time in the water.

Like Ethelda, through your challenges, may you find a way to connect with your peace and, ultimately, your power.

—ELISA BOXER

A note about the text

The more I learned about Ethelda, the more her rebellious spirit stood out.
She caused quite a stir in society by highlighting outdated laws and policies
that she believed needed to change: swimming with socks, for example, and a
lack of public pools. It was this convention-challenging nature that I wanted
to convey with the italicized thoughts and conversations in the book.
Although they are reflective of what I learned through meticulous research, the
specific italicized thoughts, conversations, and speech bubbles are works of fiction.

Selected sources online

Lord, Craig. "Ethelda Bleibtrey's Pioneering World Record 100 Years Ago This Day." 2019.
https://www.swimmingworldmagazine.com/news/ethelda-bleibtreys-pioneering-world-record-100-years-ago-this-day/

Shim, Peggy. "Meet Ethelda Bleibtrey, America's First Female Swimming Gold Medalist." 2017.
https://www.teamusa.org/News/2017/March/22/Meet-Ethelda-Bleibtrey-Americas-First-Female-Swimming-Gold-Medalist

"Ethelda Bleibtrey, American Athlete." 2022. https://www.britannica.com/biography/Ethelda-Bleibtrey

"Ethelda Bleibtrey, the trailblazer for women's swimming who was arrested due to her swimsuit." 2019.
https://www.olympic.org/news/ethelda-bleibtrey-the-trailblazer-for-women-s-swimming-who-was-arrested-due-to-her-swimsuit

"From the Archives: Swimmer who contracts polio gets Olympic chance." 2018.
https://www.timesunion.com/upstate/article/From-the-Archives-Swimmer-who-contracts-polio-12519005.php

"Ethelda Bleibtrey." PBS She Inspires series video, 1:00. First aired January 10, 2019.
https://www.pbs.org/video/ethelda-bleibtrey-she-inspires-r5jlhx/

International Swimming Hall of Fame. https://ishof.org/ethelda-bleibtrey.html

"100 Years of the Olympic Games—Antwerpen 1920." Chronos-Media History. YouTube video, 1:00:17. Posted 2014.
https://www.youtube.com/watch?v=CNTu99tunuc